T0129506

Kel's Poetry Blues

Kel's Poetry Blues

Kelton Latson

authorHOUSE®

AuthorHouse™
1663 Liberty Drive
Bloomington, IN 47403
www.authorhouse.com
Phone: 1-800-839-8640

Published by AuthorHouse   11/08/2012

ISBN: 978-1-4772-8785-9 (sc)
ISBN: 978-1-4772-8811-5 (e)

Library of Congress Control Number: 2012920842

Dancing in your eyes

It's never a surprise that every time I see you I find myself dancing in your eyes.
Whether it's fast dancing or slow dancing,
it always leads to something romancing.
All I wanna do is cool out and relax outside with you by my side.
Being held hostage by your smile and watch me dancing in your eyes.
While I hold your hands feeling your soft sun-kissed skin,
I'll be staring into your beautiful eyes, watching us dance.

Poetry

Some write about being mad, some write about being sad. Some write about the feeling of really hating their dad. Some write about being young, some write about being grown. Some write about being alone, some write about never finding home. Some write about the cause, some write about the struggle. Some write about the bully at school giving them trouble. Some write about politics, some write about religion. Some write about having a lack of faith,

Some write about having a vision. Some write about failing schools, some write about being used. Some write about being in love, and some write about playing the fool. Some write about the moon, some write about the stars. Some write about how they have yet to discover who they really are. Some write about the mountains, some write about sun. Some write about giving the world the number one. Some write about going against the grain, some write about the pain. Some write about going outside just to sing in the rain. Some write about their dream man, some write about their dream girl. Some write about their dreamland, some write about their dream world. Most just write about the dream. Some write about their romantic feelings and how they got it really bad. Some write about the one person they wished they could of had. I write about it all, cus this is my journey and I got a window seat. Any and every thing, that's the true meaning of poetry.

Everyday People

Everyday people,
laugh and smile,
Everyday people,
all in the crowd.
Everyday people cry when sad,
Everyday people rage when mad.
Everyday people with emotion they scream,
everyday people filled with hopes and dreams.
Everyday people we love and hate,
everyday people look for love then wait.
Everyday people make foolish mistakes,
but everyday people get chances for a clean slate.
Though sometimes everyday people never realize what they're doin,
everyday people still realize they're only human.

All I do is write good people

All I do is write poems. I write poems about feeling sad, mad, happy and sometimes about being alone. All I do is write poems. That's all I ever done, that's all I ever do, and I don't just write them for me, but I write them for you. I wrote poems for you because I thought that you would want them, I thought that you would need them, because they always put a smile on your face every time you read them. And at that time when I met you, you were sad, lonely, down in the dumps and the clouds above your head were dark. So I thought that a little poem would cause a spark, a spark of joy. A spark of sunshine so it can shake being sad and let happiness takes its place. And after you read it you smiled and then I smiled, and we both had smiles on our faces. It made me feel good inside that I could make you feel good inside. Because all along I knew the good person that you are. And there is nothing wrong with that, because being a good person can take you far. There is never anything wrong about being good to somebody, because a good person is good for everybody. Whether it's a good man, good woman, good boy or girl. It feels good to be around good people because there aren't many in the world. And that's what I love about poetry, because God gave me a gift to use good fulfilling words to uplift you and me. And this is all I do, all I ever wanna do, is to write poems about how there is so much good, in you.

4

Can you smile

Can you smile for me lady, cus it builds up my spirit. It plays a joyful song and I can't wait to hear the lyrics. Can you smile for me lady, cus It has me hypnotize, and every time I get to see it, it makes me feel good inside. Can you smile for me lady, cus I don't think you know what it can do? The joy in your smile brings out all the good in you. Can I hold your hand while you smile? Just to see if it makes you hold your smile longer.

Friendship slowly builds, but a smile of affection and gentle touch makes the connection stronger. Will you let me make you smile? Cus I wanna do it whenever. Cus when you smile, I smile, and together I hope we smile forever.

Boys and Girls

Girl in all red, dreams about tomorrow.
Girl in all blue, as liquor to drown her sorrow.
Boy in all green has no hope or faith.
Boy in all gray prays that joy will stay.
Girl in all purple holds fast to her dreams.
Boy in all orange strives to succeed.
All the girls work hard, never getting any slack.
All the boys teach each other,
but wished daddy came back.
Girl and boy look in the mirror looking at the man and woman there.
They're roses bloomed from stone, though nobody else cares.

Do you see the pride in the mother

Do you see the pride in the mother who sings her own struggling life songs,
goes through parenthood all alone,
but still manages to stay strong.
Do you see the pride in the mother who knows her young so well,
she guides them down a path to make sure they never fail?
Do you see the pride in the mother that sheds so many tears, that it can
create a river that can flow forever, but with her strong son by her side
we can flow in it together.

In So Deep

You in too deep ,
so deep into the swirl,
deep inside your thoughts,
too deep for this world.
Losing touch from all the shine,
so deep into time.
Your strong deep thoughts,
too much for weak minds.
You encourage them speak,
encourage them to think.
Doesn't seem like enough,
you just in so deep.
Eventually they will crown you,
and quickly they will dethrone you.
Don't understand how you think,
they will disown you.
Too deep for everyday people,
so deep into the swirl,
So deep into life,
you too deep for this world.
Stay deep inside yourself,
that's how you stay true.
Don't try to save the world,
cus it ain't tryna save you.

All kinds of blue

My horn plays the blues,
my poetry writes the blues.
Lonely girl sings the blues,
lonely boy hides the blues.
The blues cause pain and it all feels the same.
The blue supreme continues to reign and the blues lets it rain.
But the blue rain don't fall from the sky,
it falls from our eye.
Blue teary river never lets our face stay dry.
The blues got us all sad and so sad we do get.
Feeling all kinds of blue we forget what happy is.

Just like daddy

So bitter and cold just like daddy.
No confidence or faith just like daddy.
You not brave just afraid just like daddy.
Full of lies and excuses just like daddy.
Boy you not wise just yet,
you're still young, dumb and stupid, just like daddy.
I tell ya, you better get that hatred out yo heart boy or you gon be just
another nigga. Just like daddy.

Love like this

When we love like this hearts connect and don't miss.
Creating a strange feeling we never do forget.
When we love like this we take that risk.
Holding hands under the moonlight in the late night mist.
When we love like this we gently touch lips.
Creating a bond forever off of one sweet kiss.

Dream Stuck

Everything feels right and things are looking bright,
soaring high into the sky feeling so fly.
Grasping everything around me letting nothing pass me by,
all in my mind everything is all mines.
Not a doubt or a worry everything is just fine.
Only in this image can I make it this far.
Slow dancing on the moon hang gliding off the stars.
I wish it was all real cus it's not what it seems.
Nothing sucks worse than to be stuck in a dream.

Wishing Stars

Sittin under the moonlight on the late night.
Amazed how every single star shines so bright.
Sittin here by myself, nobody by my side on the hill top lookin up at the clear blue sky.
While I sit on this high mount, I began to count.
Every one of them has a meaning, not a worry or a doubt.
Making all kinds of wishes praying that they'll come.
It's just too many stars in the sky to just wish on only one.

Maybe Tomorrow

Maybe tomorrow, when the sky is once blue,
and the sun shines again,
when everything is refreshed,
and a new day begins.
When all sorrows are left behind,
and placed in the past.
When we can enjoy ourselves
and smile,
be with friends
and can laugh. When we finally realize that time doesn't wait,
dump the heavy loads of worries
and start with a clean slate.
When we finally receive all the love that we give,
maybe tomorrow, we can finally start to live.

Mr. Sandman

Mr. Sandman, don't bring the world your dream.

Cus they'll shoot them down quick if they don't understand what they mean.

Mr. Sandman, you better keep your dreams to yourself, cus they don't value anything to anybody else.

Mr. Sandman, your dreams you shouldn't bother to share.

There's not a naysayer who won't say no or an indifferent person who won't say they don't care. Mr. Sandman, keep all your dreams astray and never draw them in the sand or they'll get washed away.

Eyes

Your eyes tell a story with a setting and a plot.
It tells where you been and what you been through,
who you forgave and who you forgot.
Your eyes scream happiness, but you felt the pain.
And whenever your eyes felt sadness they tend to let it rain.
Your eyes sing a song with lyrics that are meaningful.
Singing from the heart coming straight from the soul.
Some think they know beauty.
Some don't know it at all.
But when I look at you your eyes tell it all.
At night there is no reason to look for shining stars in the skies,
because all the sparkle and shine comes from your eyes.

All dreams go blue

—⌘—

All dreams go green
cus they go, go, go.
They just keep on going sometimes you won't even know.
All dreams go yellow
cus eventually they take caution
and then slow down.
The dream slowly starts to fade and so does the people
who were once around.
All dreams go red
cus once you think you're half way to the top
there's always something that causes you to stop.
But where do dreams go after they all been deferred?
After they all been shatter and kicked to the curb.
They all go to this woeful place, a sad mind state.
When dreams are no longer held by the beholder and convinced
that they're over and can no longer come true.
All dreams must go.
All dreams go blue.

Girl Blue

If I could rewind time,
I'd start with girl blue,
and maybe this time
we could be one instead of two.
If I could try again with girl blue,
maybe, just maybe her feelings would come through.
It seems just like yesterday when I was staring into girl blue's eyes,
and my young heart skipped a beat the first time she said hi.
I've moved on from girl blue now and I've learned to forget her,
but when I look at old pictures,
I know that I'll always miss her.
If I could rewind time, I'd give my
chances another try,
and this time I won't be so quick to say goodbye.
If I could rewind time, I'd start again with girl blue,
and maybe, just
maybe it will all come true.

Lonely girl, lonely girl always faking her happiness.
Lonely girl, lonely girl I can see how sad you get.
Lonely girl, lonely girl life is hard to enjoy.
Lonely girl, lonely girl even the finer things can't fill the void.
Lonely girl, lonely girl, nobody by her side.
Lonely girl, lonely girl, her smile screams cry, cry, cry.
Lonely girl don't need money.
Lonely girl don't need a car.
Lonely girl don't need fame or to be treated like a star.
Lonely girl needs affection.
Lonely girl needs love.
Lonely girl, lonely girl I can understand your sorrow.
Lonely girl I promise, you won't be lonely tomorrow.

Shining stars,
blue sky,
blue hill,
where the blues cry.
Yearning for love
on a blue day,
trapped feelings,
so the blues stay.
Blue thought
on the blue train,
blue harmony,
the blues sang.
Blue journey,
blue life,
quick blue days,
endless blue nights.
The blue is never over,
the blue is never through.
My creative blue world
made by Kel Blue.

What's a dreams biggest nightmare?
Is it when all hopes for that dream suddenly disappear?
Is it when the chances of that dream ever happening becomes very rare?
What's a dreams biggest nightmare?
Is it when the dream no longer matters?
Is it when you place the dream inside a glass jar and it shatters?
What's a dreams biggest nightmare?
Is it when the dream loses its hold?
Is it when the dream squares up and starts to fold?
Maybe it's when the dream is stuck in empty hallways and has to watch all open doors close. Maybe it's when the once believer in the dream no longer came through,
or is it when the dream is told that it will never come true?
What's a dreams biggest nightmare?

The boy who could

The boy heard he doesn't.
The boy heard he won't.
The boy heard the doubts, which took away his clout.
The boy said he can but all he heard was he can't.
He no longer knew if he would,
cus it's placed in his mind that he wouldn't.
He always thought he could, but all he ever heard was he couldn't.

At night while I'm sleepin
there you go creepin.
Into the night and I wonder what you are seekin.
Creepin into this fantasy where you are always found.
It feels as if you wanna runaway but you still stick around.
Your smile is filled with such joy and grace.
I wish I could see you smile while I'm awake.
But when my eyes open wide you always disappear
and when my eyes shut for a rest you are always there.
At night when I'm sleepin
there you go creepin.
Why must it be that you always creep?
Creepin while I'm sleep.
Creepin into my dreams.

I once knew a dream Just like I once knew a friend.
It came unexpected
so I had no clue on when it would end.
When I dream about my dream it was all fun and play.
I stood by my dream not caring about what others say.
My dream had confidence but at times it would shake.
I keep encouraging my dream so people's words wouldn't cause it to break.
My dream shed tears, but it also cracked smiles.
Sometimes it would work, but sometimes the tears kept it down.
My dream wrote to me once saying it isn't where it wanted to be.
My dream was a wish with a plan, but the plan didn't involve me.
I never stopped dreaming about my dream because I'm still dreamin.
But maybe my dream is something that is hard to believe in.
So I once saw a dream just like I once saw a stranger.
I made eye contact like I already knew it, smiled and said hi.
And just like a stranger it passed me on by.

Still dreaming

Still thinkin about the day we finally met.
I'm still thinkin about those love poems I wrote, all of them which she kept.
Still hearing her voice, the sweetness in her talk.
Still visualizing her entrance into my world, such confidence in her walk.
I'm still hearing her name when the cold wind blows.
Still thinkin of her smile when I see the biggest stars glow.
I still remember the hugs.
I still remember the kiss.
I still remember the feeling of touching those soft, warm and juicy lips.
I still remember the laughs.
I still remember the cries.
I still remember the day when she said goodbye.
Though she took her love away and the happiness as deferred.
Why is it that I still dream?
Still dreaming of her.

One Day she'll know,
one day she'll see.
One day she'll think,
and think of me.
One day she'll care,
one day she'll love.
One day she'll greet me and there will be plenty of kisses and plenty
of hugs.
I wish one day was here,
I wish one day was now.
One day we'll share laughs and one day we'll share smiles.
When she is in my presence,
it will be her love I'll breathe in.
I keep telling myself she'll like me,
one day it will sink in.

Her smile

I didn't see her smile today,
maybe I'll see it tomorrow.
Wishing that I can see it all the time,
maybe her smile I can borrow.
Though shyness kicks in on me and freezes me up before I can say hi,
I smile when she smiles every time she passes by.
Why does her smile seem so damn perfect?
Cus it lights up her already light face.
Or is it because her smile slows everything down even when they're in
a fast moving pace.
Why does her smile amuse me so much?
Why does her smile cause my heart to be in such a rush?
Her smile silents my mind,
and I can hear her voice telling me to hush.
Why does she smile every time she sees me?
Could she be thinkin the same thing that I think?
I don't know what it is,
but her smile drives me wild.
Maybe she's across this campus and her far away dorm,
writing about why I make her smile.

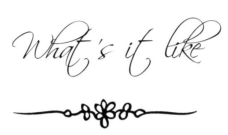

What's it like

What is it like to be with the one you like? Do you get excited when they come to sight? Is it easy to be at peace with yourself and sleep at night? Do you wake up every morning knowing today will be a good day, all because you get to see their lovely face? What's it like to be with the one you like? Knowing you took the chance when you finally got it. You have all the happiness in the world and you can't even hide it. Knowing if you didn't tell her how you felt, you would be forever haunted. But you finally build courage and now you got the girl you always wanted. What's it like to be with the one you like? She's always on your mind and you are always on hers. You show your feelings for her through actions as well as you do words. What's it like to see the one you like smile so bright? Knowing you both are the perfect fit and you match just right. What's it like to hold her in your arms and feel her smooth soft skin, kissing her lips that are filled with sweetness making a connection that'll never end. What's it like I ask? The dream girl you always wrote poems about and songs you always mention her in. You finally got the girl you dreamed about to be your girlfriend. So, tell me, what's it like? Feelings I'll never be able to show. What's it like to be with the one you like? Maybe someday I'll know.

Happy soul

You use to have a happy soul,
grinning from ear to ear,
no longer are you here
leaving my soul in tears.
You use to have a happy soul,
the brightest smile on earth,
your happiness was priceless
but it had so much worth.
You use to have a happy soul,
such a very strong heart
your joy always shined even in the dark.
Your soul is no longer here to see tomorrow.
Which means nobody is here to get my soul through sorrow.

Happy Kel, filled with joy and grace.
Mad Kel, punches everybody in the face.
Sad Kel, heart is filled with sorrow.
Suicidal Kel, doesn't see a tomorrow.
Normal Kel, nobody understands.
Lonely Kel, nobody to hold his hand.
Drunk Kel, speaks sober thoughts.
High Kel, his world gets lost.
Teary eyed Kel, only in the dark.
Creative Kel, express through art.
Serious Kel, coming straight from the heart.
Dreamy Kel, hope they don't get deferred.
Poetic Kel, the realest voice I heard.
Nice Kel, nobody cares.
Failure Kel, has nobody there.
Successful Kel , what the future holds.
People who love Kel, where did they all go?

Pretty Dandelion Girl

Pretty dandelion girl,
stick true to your roots,
rise above the ground, wipe away the frown and smile.
You may not be a rose, you may not be an orchid,
but you still stand out in your own portrait.
You are unique dandelion girl,
your stem should be filled
with tremendous joy.
Have fun, let your dreams bloom
and they shall one day come.
Soak up the sun,
soak up the world,
soak up life, pretty dandenlion girl.

Lonely Soul

No father no mother,
no sister no brother
no smiles no hugs
no friends or lover.
Not a thought or a mention
I'm all on my own.
Just a lonely soul by itself.
A soul sad and alone.

Never give up

When I was growin up
I was taught to never give up.
I'm physically strong but more importantly mentally tough.
So I never give up,
I keep on pulling through.
Keep on making good things happen and my dream will come true.
I never give up
let the positive fly with me
and negativity blow by.
Nothing can ever get me low when I'm always at an all-time high.
Never give up.
I keep the faith in me
so you should have faith in you.
Never give up
cus that's something quitters never do.

Cry

The day that you died, was the night that I cried.
I cried to the pictures that gave me thoughts.
I cried to everything that reminded me of the lost.
I wish you could take these tears I shed for you.
Instead I'm left with them and my thoughts In the dark, feeling blue.
The day that you died,
was the night that I cried.
I'mma still continue to cry.
I'mma cry and cry, from beginning to end.
Then I'mma go home alone and cry some more again.

Pain

Pain is pain,
it runs slow and deep.
It settles in on your heart
and begins to slowly sink.
The strong can fight through pain,
the weak can only try.
Some let pain out through tears,
others let it build inside.
Pain is pain,
it runs so slow and so deep.
Pain makes the best experiences
so why won't you share your pain with me.
Pain is pain,
it runs slow and deep.
Pain is temporary
so never welcome defeat.

Just you & I

One of these days, when it's just you and I, we'll lay back and watch the stars in the sky. One of these days when it's just you and I, we'll encourage each other's to achieve our dreams, continuing to strive. One of these days when it's just you and I, when one feels down the other would make our soul and sprite still feel high. I'll always believe in your dreams just like you do with mines. I have faith in you the same as you have in I.

Life is a traffic Jam

Life is a traffic jam, why rush?
It slows up the time and speeds up your mind,
making you shout what the fuck.
Everybody is rushin to this,
that and the third.
Police sirens,
cars beepin,
screamin voices dyin to be heard.
Feels like too much time in life,
but not enough life in time.
Stuck in life's traffic and it feels like a non-moving line.
Since we got plenty of time on our hands in this traffic jam,
might as well regain control.
Let your mind go free,
that's something life's traffic can't hold.

Sadness in the poet

Someone shake the sadness out the poet, so he can write his motives and thoughts down pain free. So he can have confidence again and once again express in peace. Someone shake the sadness out the poet, so he can smile and never frown with his head down again. So he can see that the storm never last forever and that it will eventually end. Someone shake the sadness out the poet, let him know he has a true friend that cares. Though times always seem rough, he has a friend that's there. Someone shake the sadness out the poet, so he can get back on his feet. He always writes about being strong, but every day he feels defeat. Someone shake the sadness out the poet, shake the sadness out the poet. He talks like he's happy, but inside he's sad in the world doesn't know it. Please, someone shake the sadness out the poet.

Hold Fast to dreams

Hold fast to your dreams, Never let them die. Be free in the mind and soul, and to your dreams you should fly .Hold fast to your dreams, have goals and a plan. Believe that you will. Believe that you can. Hold fast to your dreams, though they may come slow. Be patient with your dreams, and never let them go.

Blinded Reflection of yourself

Don't be blinded, don't be blinded. Don't be blinded by the close minded. Don't be blinded by the absents of love, don't be blinded by the bait. Don't be blinded by the envy, don't be blinded by the hate. Don't be blinded by the greed that is known to corrupt man. Don't be blinded by the negativity, for it only has hateful plans. Don't be blinded by the false messages in certain songs and movies. Don't be blinded by the media and its own perception of beauty. Don't be blinded by those that say they know, but are really unsure and aware. Don't be blinded by false actions of those who only pretend to care. Don't be blinded by the media's foolery, the false actions they try to expose. Don't be blinded by false imagery that is simply designed to keep the mind closed. Don't be blinded by the evil seed that has hatched inside the hearts of those who have found it. Don't be blinded by every live action, unspoken words are usually the loudest. Don't be blinded by the perception of being someone else. Don't be blinded, so blinded to a point where you can't see the real reflection of yourself.

Love age

He say she say, we don't know love.
She say, he say we have yet to grow up.
He say, she say we way too young.
She say he say, we just a little sprung.
I say we just, not listen to what they say.
Cus you and I know love has no age.

Think about you

Do you think about me like I think about you?
It's okay if you don't, but I'll smile even more if you do.
Do I give you good impressions like you give to me?
they make me think of you often, everyday honestly.
it's okay if you don't, if your feelings aren't the same.
I just hope one day your feelings will soon change.
Hopefully that day will come, I believe it will come too.
The day you start thinking about me, just how I think about you.

The good guy

It's always tough sharing feelings when her feelings aren't the same.
I keep a little jar of confidence hoping her feelings change.
Don't know if she'll ever like me,
don't know if she even cares.
Just want her to notice me,
and realize that I'm here.
Though it's always the same result then,
not sure how it will end now.
So I smile all the time I naturally do it when she's around.
I hope one day she 'll realize
I hope she'll finally see.
The guy that's I truly am,
the good guy inside of me.

Sleeping Man

Sleeping man
you can sleep all day
but your dream won't come.
You can sleep all night
but your dream is still on the run.
Sleeping man better wake up
and go chase those dreams
or let them sink down a drain
and then they'll be no such thing.
Time to wake up sleeping man
and get the dream chasin on a roll
cus when you wake up too late
you're gonna wonder where did they all go.

Sick of writing sad poems

Sick of writing sad poems,
sick of the same song.
Something always feels like its missing
and that feeling is always strong.
Sick of writing the same situation,
sick of writing the same sad news,
Sick of writing every night on how I ended up with the blues.
Sick of writing sad poems,
sick of the same song.
Can't never get too happy
because something good always seems to go wrong.
Sick of sad poems
and the sad poems I like.
Sick of all the sad poems that I still continue to write.

She's such an actress

She's such an actress,
fake laugh,
fake smile,
faking happiness when she's really sad and ready to cry,
looking live but really dies in the inside.
She's a great actress,
been a great one for a long time.
Sometimes I don't know if she's afraid to express what's in heart or her
mind.
She just goes with the flow pretending as if I don't know.
She's such an actress but eventually she'll know and see
that she can be real with me,
be real with life,
and be real with herself,
so she can stop being such an actress.

Flossie
comeback flossie,
don't you know that we want you
and need you?
Don't you know our love for you was true
and still is too?
Flossie
comeback flossie,
don't you miss us
like we miss you?
Don't you still love us?
Flossie why did you go away?
Home is with us
this is where you're supposed to stay.
Flossie,
comeback flossie,
did we do something wrong?
Cus you been gone too long.
I wish I was at this new place that you call home.

The Blues

The blues sound so good to the ears
but feels so sad to the heart.
The blues will have you weepin
and whining alone in the deep blue shadows of the dark.
But if you're creative,
the blues will make you create
such wonderful art.
Everything blue and sad,
sad stories,
sad songs,
sad letters,
sad poems.
Everything is so blue
but its so sad.
The creation of it is good
but it still feels bad.
So what you gon do creative person?
I say you keep doing what you do.
Sing,
dance,
draw
and write the blues
until your feeling blue is through.

Little Young Blues Boy

Little young blues boy be writing his life, sketching out his day and then painting in his night. Sitting in a quiet room collecting all of his thoughts, writes them all in his pad, because he don't want them to get lost. Little young blues boy, somebody who stands out and unique, always writing about his hardships, he wants you to feel his adversity. But he don't welcome in defeat, he don't bother to weep. He just turns to his heart, and lets his soul speak. Little young blues boy, only twenty years old, maturing for a while but still got more time to grow. Though he sings the same tune about the old weary blues, he recites it with passion that makes the heart move. I look forward to seeing little young blues boy at all the open mics, I hope he recites my favorite poem tonight. He be writin for the world, so world pay attention. I be writing for the mind, so let your mind listen.

Kelton Latson, a native from Cleveland Ohio started writing his freshmen year in high school. He has truly embraced his talent of creative writing after being encouraged by his high school literature teacher, after she read lyrics to a song that Kelton had written. It was then, when Kelton started writing poetry and performing spoken word in front of crowds. Kelton's talent of poetry writing and reciting would eventually lead to him winning a scholarship to attend Kent State University. Eventually, Kelton's love for urban fictional literature books grew, and he begin to develop a huge interest for them. Some of his favorite urban fictional writers include Omar Tyree, Eric Jerome Dickey and Angela Johnson. Kelton is a very inspired, young writer who hopes to have great success with his writings, and plans to forever do what he truly loves most, and that is to write.

Printed in the United States
By Bookmasters